HERMIT CRABS

by Michèle Dufresne

Pioneer Valley Educational Press, Inc.

Here is a **hermit crab.**

A hermit crab lives in a **shell**.

The hermit crab is getting
too big for its shell.
It is looking for a bigger **home**.

Look! The hermit crabs
find a cookie.
They are eating the cookie.

Hermit crabs can be little.

Hermit crabs can be big.

13

Hermit crabs can be pets.
Do you have a hermit crab?

HERMIT CRABS

hermit crab

home

shell